Let Us Start the Conversation

RAE REYNOLDS

BALBOA.PRESS

A DIVISION OF HAY HOUSE

Balboa Press books may be ordered through booksellers or by contacting:

Balboa Press
A Division of Hay House
1663 Liberty Drive
Bloomington, IN 47403
www.balboapress.com
844-682-1282

Because of the dynamic nature of the Internet, any web addresses or links contained in this book may have changed since publication and may no longer be valid. The views expressed in this work are solely those of the author and do not necessarily reflect the views of the publisher, and the publisher hereby disclaims any responsibility for them.

The author of this book does not dispense medical advice or prescribe the use of any technique as a form of treatment for physical, emotional, or medical problems without the advice of a physician, either directly or indirectly. The intent of the author is only to offer information of a general nature to help you in your quest for emotional and spiritual well-being. In the event you use any of the information in this book for yourself, which is your constitutional right, the author and the publisher assume no responsibility for your actions.

Any people depicted in stock imagery provided by Getty Images are models, and such images are being used for illustrative purposes only. Certain stock imagery © Getty Images.

Print information available on the last page.

ISBN: 979-8-7652-4636-8 (sc)
ISBN: 979-8-7652-4638-2 (hc)
ISBN: 979-8-7652-4637-5 (e)

Library of Congress Control Number: 2023919715

Balboa Press rev. date: 11/03/2023

for my son

Contents

Introduction

I have had the desire to write this book for a very long time; I did not know if it was going to be a memoir, autobiography, or a story loosely based on my life experiences. I don't think this book is any of those. We all have a journey, and at some time in our lives, it may become a healing journey. Most of us at some point in our lives are brought to our knees by this crazy thing called life. I want to share with you how I got back up, and I hope that my words might help you feel not so alone.

It does not matter what brings you to your knees but how you get back up that counts. If you can do this with love and kindness toward yourself, the transition will go much smoother. I will talk a lot about love as we go forward, so let me define what love means to me. Unconditional love is without conditions, without judgement but with empathy, respect, kindness, nurturing, forgiveness, well-being, and compassion for yourself. Learning to know yourself, the good, the bad, and the ugly truths about who you are, and accepting and embracing yourself regardless, knowing that every day you will strive to unconditionally love and forgive yourself to become a better version of yourself. You are worth this process; do not give up. If you slip, get back up again and again until you realize you are here for a reason, and that is to be just you. Once you have learned to love yourself, then you can love others.

Let me take a moment to introduce myself; I am Rae, I am a woman, an old soul, a mother, a survivor, a warrior, a therapist, someone who has listened to stories from many. I grew up in fear and trauma, which made me highly aware of my surroundings. I am a voyeur of life.

I would like to take this opportunity to invite you into my journey and the things I have learned along the way in hope that it inspires you to listen to your own heart on your journey of self and love.

The Person in the Glass

When you get what you want in your struggle for self,

And the world makes you president for a day,

Just go to the mirror and look at yourself

And see what *that* person has to say.

For it isn't your partner or family or friend

Whose judgement upon you must pass.

The person whose verdict counts the most in the end

Is the one staring back through the glass.

Some people may think you a straight-shooting chum

And call you a person of place,

But the person in the glass says you're only a bum

If you can't look that person straight in the face.

That's the person to please, never mind all the rest,

For they are with you clear up to the end,

And you've passed your most dangerous, difficult test

If that person in the glass is your friend.

You may fool the whole world down the pathway of years,

And get pats on the back as you pass,

But your final reward will be heartaches and tears

If you've cheated the person in the glass.

CHAPTER 1

Women—Generational Karma

Every woman is born with all the egg she will ever have. What that means is that you were inside your mother and she was in your grandmother and so on. This statement means far more than the simple words—you were part of the woman carrying you before you were ever conceived. Cells have memory, emotional and physical, so all the things your mother, and also your grandmother, went through from birth are inside of you. As women, we carry a lot of baggage that is not necessarily ours to carry. Through cellular memory and learned behavior, we have access to the process we need to truly figure out who we are. Your soul is a different entity than your physical being. The question is, Are we a soul with a human body or are we a body with a soul?

Are you the physical, are you the spiritual, or are you both? So we must figure out who we are amongst all of that. This is what the journey is all about.

It's time that women start taking back their power. Become individuals. The human race would not survive without women, and we need to start to realize our own worth. Becoming yourself on your journey is key at any stage of your existence. Most men could not juggle their lives without women or a good partner to help them enjoy their own journey.

I am going to use women as an example here. Now that we are trying to be equal to men, we are taking on more and more roles in life—we are partners, mothers, professionals, and we engage in leisure activities and exercise to stay fit. We are filling our bowls to the brim. We never give ourselves down time to allow ourselves to heal from our days. Juggling everything is stressful, no matter how well you do it. Most women are the worst at looking after themselves, for they are constantly looking after everyone else— this is part of our learned behavior.

The reason I am writing this book is to show that we can heal ourselves. I am fifty-one years old. I have a few select women I would call my friends. The rest would rather use you, stab you in the back, judge you, or be two-faced toward you. These types of women I have met time and again. Therefore, I am writing this book. Ladies, it is time to turn the mirror around. If you have agreed with any of the issues I have discussed so far, it is time to turn the mirror back on yourself. Time to rethink your own insecurities around these issues. I am not saying that everyone has to like one another, but just because someone is not your cup of tea does not give you the right to treat people like this. Especially women. We should be supporting one another, building one another up, not bringing one another down. For if there is anyone who can empathize with a woman, it should be another woman. We know what we can and do each and every day. We can understand what it is like to be mothers, partners, daughters, sisters, coworkers, and so on. We all go through first kisses, first romantic encounters, and many of us become first-time mothers. Instead of understanding or empathizing, we tend to belittle or judge others, and for what? We do it for the attention of men, the attention of anyone. Instead, we should pick others up and support others with compassion, empathy, and understanding. If bad things are not happening to you, they could be happening to your friends, your daughters. Women are jealous of other women. Someone may be prettier or have a nicer figure. I can tell you that being pretty is not always a good thing. There have been many times over the course of my life when I wished I was unattractive.

Some men see an attractive woman, and right away, they think she cannot be very smart and is just there for their entertainment. If you are pretty, they want you there for sex. Remember that beauty is in the eye of the beholder, and if two people are meant to be together, it will not matter what you look like to anyone else.

You can't keep looking for acceptance from others if you can't accept yourself.

It is time that women step into their own power as a collective. Even though we have burned our bras, are able to vote, and have equal rights, we are still missing something. I believe that what we miss is that this planet cannot survive without us. That is the power of self as women. I said before, why are we trying to become equal to men? That is just a sacrificed woman. Women are everything. We give life, we nurture, we refer to Mother Earth, and we are sacred beings; it is time that we truly embrace our essence. We are multitaskers—the list is endless. We keep sacrificing ourselves to men, when in fact men cannot live without us. (I apologize that this is not politically correct verbiage.) The human race would not succeed if it was not for women. We all need to wrap our heads around this. A woman's journey is her own, as is everyone's. If you are content with being at home raising your kids or being a powerhouse at your profession, own your shit and run with it. If it becomes unsatisfying, then change it. Change allows us to grow and not stagnate. Keep learning, keep pushing yourself to be a better version of yourself, no matter what that looks like. Your existence on this beautiful planet does not have to look like anyone else's. It's time to embrace our differences and unite with one purpose, and that is to support Mother Earth. It is a time for peace and love to ignite this planet. It is time that women come out of their slumber and start to lead and forge a new path for all of existence. I focus on women, for we tend to be more emotional and practical. It is time for us to put our heads together to redefine this planet's future.

Working together will unite women on a completely different level. Taking the reins from men to make this planet thrive is a united front that we should all embrace. Healing ourselves will in turn heal her. Women are beautiful, nurturing beings, and once the pangs of love resonate within you, you will want to share that with all living entities in this universe. The strength in women is not shared by men. We are mysterious creatures all to ourselves, and we forget that. Men have made this society about greed, gluttony, power, and destruction. Mother Nature is returning the favor of destruction; she is creating storms and climate change so that we will take notice. And we are not. Men keep making power about ownership and borders.

CHAPTER 2

My Journey

Don't let your past own you; own your past.

My journey in search of myself has been a story and a half. We all have a story, and yours will look different from mine. However, there are situations that we all go through. Our first loves, breakups, the death of our parents, death of loved ones, and so on. It is the stuff in between that may be different, and that is OK, for we are not all meant to look the same or have the same journey.

My journey did not start well. I was conceived in rape and domestic violence. My mother chose to give me life, and I am forever grateful for this. I was brought up in fear, anger, and resentment. Unconditional love was not on the table for me. I was born to parents with their own issues, ones that went back for generations.

My whole life has been a healing journey, again something that I am grateful for otherwise I would not be here writing this book. Growing up in fear and without a lot of guidance has made me live by my intuition, not that I always listened to her (my soul). This is not the story of my life, all my good and bad choices, but about learning to love myself unconditionally. When I was younger, my only dream was to be happy. I kept looking, running, and chasing what I thought would make me happy. I went to college thinking that being a professional would be the answer or having a stable relationship, somebody to love me. Buying my first home, then materialistic possessions became my goals, but I did not find happiness in any of these things. Believe me: I had a lot of fun doing all these things, but none of them really made me feel whole.

Until the day I had my son, and I learned to love someone else unconditionally. I figured out that I did not want to keep making the same mistakes. But I did make the mistakes, and I hit my bottom. I was alone, unhappy. I had just come out of a very toxic relationship, but I realized, at the time, that it was not the relationship I had with my partner—it was the one I had with myself.

I was at the lowest point of my life. My relationship ended, my mother had just passed away, I was unhappy, and I was in a toxic place within myself. I realized that I had to turn the mirror around. What was the common denominator in my life? Me. I realized that I was seeking happiness outside of myself, and the way I was going about it was not making me happy at all. I knew I needed to quit drinking, for this was a coping mechanism that I learned from my parents, and it was no longer working for me. I was now using alcohol to numb everything, to deaden all the feelings I had related to my breakup, the death of my mother, and my loneliness. This one thing (alcohol) is what screwed up my own childhood, and I did not want it to mess up my son's. It took me about a year and a half to completely quit drinking. I have been sober for over five years. This has been accomplished one breath, one step, one moment at a time. I have never missed the alcohol, and I realized that when I was drinking, I made all the wrong decisions in my life. That third drink permeates the judgement center of your brain.

I realized that I had to figure out why I was drinking in the first place and all the reasons why it became a crutch. If you truly want to quit an addiction, you must figure out the psychological reasons why you are addicted in the first place. Why are you swallowing/numbing your emotions? And what with?

I started changing my life patterns; I started walking my dog every day, cooking all our meals, filling my time while my son was in school. I did also decide to go to therapy with a clinical therapist when I first started my healing journey to make sure I was on the right path, not only for myself but for my son too. He was being impacted as well; he'd just lost his grandmother and stepfather. I realized I was the only one who could navigate that path for the both of us. I knew I had to be very mindful, there was no room for failure for me because of my son. I wanted to protect him from me ever slipping backward.

The first thing I did was to start to trust myself again to make the right decisions for myself. Which in turn meant making the right decisions for my son. This one thing was my first major step and would help build my inner confidence. I also realized I needed to retrain my brain to have a more positive outlook on myself; I needed to change the narrative. I was no longer the victim of my parents or my situation.

To look at the big picture here, I not only lived through my own childhood trauma but that of my mother's as well. Learned behavior was passed down one generation to the next. Go back and read the first sentences of this book—it was a game changer to let that sink in. As women, we are incredible; we carry the lineage through time. To be able to come to terms with that and realize the magnitude of that knowledge is incredible. You will get there too.

All this coincided with the death of my mother, whom I had a complex relationship with. In the end, I tried to understand her and the effect she had on my life. I realized that I needed to find my own self-worth, to love and nurture myself for the first time, to rebirth myself as me, without someone else's baggage. To heal my inner child, learning to trust, nurture, respect, accept, and love myself without conditions became my goal. I learned that I could change myself through growth and love.

I had to figure out what I needed to feel nurtured and why. What was the hurt that I needed to heal? Was this hurt related to abandonment, lack of worth, living in fear? Turning all the negatives into positives—I was alive, I had my son and my dog. Walking my dog in nature was the most healing thing I have done for myself. It allowed me to connect with nature, with myself. There was a ravine by my house that lead to the water; along the path there was a fork that went either into the bush or to a clearing.

I would at first choose the clearing, for I could see what was in front of me. It took me about three weeks to be able to go through the forest.

Thank God I did. There was a creek and a path that followed it up a hill, over bridges until you came to the water. It was magnificent, and totally what I needed. My dog loved it. This was my time to think and process everything and put it into perspective. Sure, I did not always make the best decisions, but I was on the road to changing that. Learning to only do things that I wanted to do, that made me feel good with myself. I also wrote letters to myself, my mother, my ex, my dad, and all the negatives that had been in my life. I made a little ritual of burning the letters and realized I needed to let my past go in order to walk a new path that was my own.

Believe me: this was very scary, but I knew that I was worth it. My goal became to heal myself to protect my son. It was a perfect time in my life; I was living in a town where I did not know anybody. Within six months, I started a new path in my career and was looking after my son and me.

I knew that I was put on this earth to spread love but had to teach myself what that meant. We are in a society that is so far removed from what love is that it is mind-blowing.

I am sure that there are people out there that are living in a place filled with love, but unfortunately, they are few and far between.

I was not conceived out of love, nor was I brought up in a loving environment. My mother resented me, and my father was a workaholic, an alcoholic for the first eight years of my life, and absent for the next eight years.

I should really spend a whole chapter on my parents, but the bits and pieces of my life are not relevant. We all have our issues; I do not want any of us to compare notes. I wrote this book to put into words my experiences, to help others not feel alone with their problems. I want them to realize that it is OK to not fit into a box. Many of us have some similar situations, and I know you can make it through with love in your heart.

I learned in my early twenties that I could not blame my dysfunctional childhood for everything, that I had to take responsibility for who I was. I needed to shed my skin of the scared little girl and move forward. It is amazing to look back from where I am today. I am very grateful for the journey.

As a child, I never fit in, not in my family nor with my peers. At times, I felt invisible and that no one really saw me. I knew I was a strong individual but kept looking for acceptance from others.

I have overcome my own fears, for I know in past lives I have been killed or exiled due to my differences as a healer, an intuitive, a strong independent woman in times when we were taught to shut up and just fit in and not speak of our differences. These are the layers that as modern women we need to shed to embrace our inner powers as women.

I want to talk about recognizing patterns in your own situation. Familial patterns are learned behaviors, mannerisms, and characteristics we as little sponges pick up during our childhood. Tendencies can be passed down from generation to generation. Most of these patterns have something to do with the relationships our mothers and parental figures were in, how they treated others, and how they responded to situations. The most important thing to look at is how your parents treated you. As children, we have nothing to compare our parents' behavior to; I did not even realize until age eight that my parents favored one of my siblings over me. As I said earlier, some of us are lucky to have parents that love us unconditionally, but most parenting is influenced by how well you behave or what you achieve. None of us are taught to love ourselves unconditionally. On a side note, I think one of the most detrimental things you can do with your kids is to compare them to yourself. Let your children blossom into themselves; unless you are perfect, we do not need two of you. Children should be seen for themselves, not who we want them to be.

Realizing that we all have issues, and that our parents had issues as well, is huge and the beginning of your own path to becoming an individual.

Learning to nurture yourself, trusting yourself to make the right decisions is important. You must give yourself time to think about what you truly want out of this life as opposed to what everyone else wants for you.

I grew up in fear, anger, and negativity. For most of my adult life, I concentrated on school and having fun, but I was running from whom I was. I was being someone that I was not, to fit in. For this is how women are conditioned; I ran from what was the norm—to get married and have babies and be domesticated. I did not have my son until I was thirty-seven.

The darkest part of my life started after my dad passed away. The longer I did not deal with my grief, the worse it got. Then things just kept building. I was in a toxic relationship, and I was more focused on fixing my partner than I was on fixing myself. Then my mother got sick and passed away rather suddenly. My relationship with my mother had been very troubled; I needed to resolve issues around abandonment and not being wanted. As I said before, part of myself had to die along with my parents. The scared little girl who was always trying to be perfect, the one who was always trying to please everyone by herself. This is the image that I saw in the mirror. I knew then that it was time to let her go. For me, she was self-destroying; I no longer wanted or needed her in my life. I had built an alter ego to deal with all the trauma that I had been through. I was the woman who did not give a shit, so that no one could ever hurt me again. There are so many things I had to realize—that vulnerability was OK, that there was even a word for it. I had to teach myself to feel emotions, having my son helped me a lot in this department. Before my son, I was living on autopilot.

As I started to nurture my inner child and myself, I figured out things like acceptance, self-worth, unconditional love for myself, empathy, all these things I had never allowed myself to feel or experience. So many of us are taught to suck it up, not to cry, not to show feelings. Truly getting to know yourself is one of the greatest gifts that you can give yourself and to your loved ones around you.

As I said before, I have a few select friends, but I really have stopped putting myself out there to meet new people. It is so hard to find the people I want to meet, like finding a needle in the haystack, and I cannot be bothered anymore. Also, I have learned to love myself and to be content with my own company.

Embarking on a healing journey is not always easy. Let me tell you it can be lonely and daunting at times. I have been fortunate to have my son and my dog along for the ride. Depending on your circumstances, you might have to purge friendships and relationships, and sometimes family members. This can be difficult, but it will be worth it in the long run. Turning the mirror around on my own life, I found I was a negative entity in my own world. That was not me. I let situations bring me down. I had just come out of a very toxic relationship, one that was very familiar to me. I repeated my own pattern of my relationship with my mother. I was never good enough for her. No matter what I did, I could have done better. I tried to be perfect, but that is not an attainable lifestyle for anyone.

My father had passed away the year before. I was in a toxic relationship with a self-admitted sociopath. About two and a half years later, his father passed away. Six weeks later, my mom passed away from cancer. Her illness was quick and took my sisters and I by surprise; she was only seventy-one at the time. Six months later, my relationship ended. The demise of all these relationships turned out to be very good for me, although at the time it did not feel that way. I was alone with my son and dog in a strange town trying to pick up the pieces of my life. My drinking escalated because I was also suffering from PTSD from my relationship. I used alcohol as a coping mechanism to calm myself; this was a learned coping skill from my childhood. Believe me: I knew I had to quit, but there was so much going on I did not know where to start to put my life back together. Over the next year and half it would go in waves of me trying to control the alcohol and using it as a crutch. I did seek counselling at the time, which helped. I found a therapist through an association where I lived. My therapist suggested that I read the book *Women That Love Too Much by Robin Norwood.* The book showed me familial patterns; I knew that I had to retrain the way I was thinking and dealing with things.

For anyone who has tried to quit anything, you know it is a process. I researched AA, but their success rate was only four percent. I also knew that AA meetings became a substitute for the addiction. I realized I had to figure out why I was drinking, and I knew I was screwing up. I had pieced together that my drinking was a learned behavior. Drinking was one thing when I was single and did not have my son. I also figured out that I resented my own parents for their drinking. They never changed for us kids. I knew if I wanted to break the pattern for my son, it had to start with me. I figured out how to change my habits. I started by going for walks every day with the dog while my son was at school. I started making crafts and cooking everything from scratch to fill my days. I journaled all the time. It was one moment at a time. I was on course to figure out who I was without all the toxic relationships. I wanted to heal the relationship that I had with myself. I realized all the mistakes I had made in my life were when I was drinking. Drinking was not who I was ever meant to be. I was done with that part of my life. It was scary, for it was a major part of my life. Alcohol was always present in my life, either with my parents or family, friends, or as a social escape. All my relationships were with people who drank. Now I wanted a drama-free life. My last relationship was so stressful that I was ready for a new chapter in my life for my son and I.

I started putting the pieces of the puzzle together, and I started to see the big picture. I had never fit in, and as much as drinking was a very negative part of my childhood, in my late teens it was any easy way to fit in and find similar people.

You can't keep looking for acceptance from others, if you cannot accept yourself first. Acceptance is one of the first things you need to accomplish on your road to recovery. You must accept that you cannot change the past, but you can change your future. Accept that you have made mistakes but, you lived through them and you are here. Accept that sometimes you need to fall and get back up in order to see a better version of yourself. Accept that you must unlearn childhood behaviors and bad behaviors that have developed because of trauma. Accept that we all are a little broken and need to heal. Accept yourself for who you are right now in this moment. When I started on my own journey, there were words and emotions I did not even know existed. For I lived in fear for the most part of my life. As children, we don't know any better, we are innocent and vulnerable to our environment.

In my situation, as angry as I was that I had to deal with abandonment issues, alcohol issues, and codependency, I also had to accept the fact that even though my mother did not want me and was raped to conceive me, she still gave me life. She could have chosen to have an abortion and hightail out of the relationship with my father. She stayed and gave me life. If we take the time to self-reflect, I think we would all realize that there is a big picture for us. We are all meant to be here on this planet right now. Just as I am writing this book, you are also meant to be reading it.

I am completely ahead of myself. We need to go through the steps of self-love to see the big picture for ourselves, to step away from what we thought was expected of us and step into what we expect of ourselves. Honesty, integrity, empathy, and compassion are words that are not used enough anymore. Each step toward change for us as individuals is a giant leap toward a global entity of love and peace.

I know I am worth all the changes that I have made for myself, for I see how they have impacted my son and the way I raised him. I am by no means a perfect mother, but I am a mother that will never give up on my son or myself. I have figured out that I am here for a reason and part of that reason is writing this book so we can share and grow together. I know that life has brought me to my knees more than once, so I had to figure out how to get back up, to share that with you. We all need to make mistakes in life, but we do not need to keep making them. We do not need to stay down. You can get back up at any point in your life and make the changes for a better future for yourself. If we all start to believe in ourselves just a little bit more, start loving ourselves a little bit more for who we actually are instead of who we pretend to be—the false picture we keep portraying to the masses, this world would be an even more beautiful place.

There is a quote that I love, "That if we started seeing each other as souls, instead of just looking at our faces, this would make the world a better place" Author unknown. This is an idea that deserves more attention. Your body is strictly a vessel that carries you from birth to death, but it is your soul that gives you life in between. Tapping into your soul is the true essence of existence; connecting with your soul is the holy grail of existence. We need to get rid of the material, ego-driven existence that most of us have resigned ourselves to.

Accepting that we all need to take back our responsibility for making this planet a better place for future generations and for our future selves. Our souls are the time travelers of existence; I hope we can figure it out so there is a beautiful utopia and not a post-apocalyptic existence to look forward to for all.

The reason I don't share a lot about my past is that it is over for me. I realized I needed to make changes in myself, for myself. I don't want to stay stuck in a past self that was never supposed to be me in the first place. These are some of the steppingstones I have travelled to be me in this moment.

CHAPTER 3

Your Journey

When you start out on a healing journey, and self-reflecting on who you are and what works for you, you will have to look at the relationships that you are in as well. If you are in a toxic place, more than likely the relationships you are in are toxic as well. Like attracts like. This will come with time, and a healing journey is a process. There is no quick fix to self-improvement. It is literally one breath at a time in the beginning. When you are starting out, come up with a little mantra that you can keep repeating to yourself when negative thoughts crop up or when you are triggered by someone or a situation that you are in.

Depending on what you are dealing with, seeking some sort of therapy to get you started is a great way to begin. There is community-funded help if you cannot afford therapy or do not have medical benefits. Therapy can be with a licensed therapist, or it can involve meditation, yoga, communing with nature, journaling, or whatever resonates with you. It is a step toward changing habits and things that no longer work for you. Change it up; try something new. It does not have to be anything major, but changing bad habits, or even just changing negative thought processes, is huge. There are also lots of books out there on how you can retrain your brain. I've never read any, so I cannot suggest a specific one, for I figured out the process for myself.

If there are addictions involved, then you must figure out why you became addicted and what are the things that trigger you. If you do not deal with these issues, then the addiction will return in some shape or form.

There are no exact steps that I can outline for you, for every journey is unique to the individual. Each step you take for yourself will lead you in the right direction if you pay attention to intuition, your heart, and the universe. They will not lead you astray.

We must unlearn and relearn who we are. I have talked about turning the mirror around to heal yourself; part of this process is unlearning a lot of the things our parents taught us. We learn coping mechanisms, triggers, eating habits, and how to express or suppress emotions from our parents. We learn about relationships, how we treat ourselves, family dynamics, we can even learn our gait from them too. There are so many things that we take in like little sponges when we are children. Parents are human beings with their own learned behaviors that they pass on to their children. Unlearning these generational traits is part of the process of turning the mirror around. Realizing that you are not perfect and neither were your parents is part of the healing journey.

How we see our parents as humans depends on how honest they are with you and with themselves. There are a lot of people that hide their idiosyncrasies from themselves and from the ones around them. We are taught to hide whatever is viewed as different and against societal norms. Your own self-reflection and learning to love yourself will open your eyes to many things around you. As children, we seek love and attention from our parents, and some are willing to do almost anything to get it. Again, this is a self-learned behavior. If you must act negatively to gain attention from your parents, the behavior will carry with you. As an adult, you will repeat the pattern with your peers. If there is favoritism among siblings, you will probably feel inferior to your peers down the road.

Coping mechanisms are a learned behavior. If your parents stress, eat, drink, gamble, and so on to deal with day-to-day living, these are ways you will deal with future stress. Even your gait can be learned. If you see your mom tiptoeing around to placate an angry partner or accommodate someone that works shift work, these are learned behaviors. If your parents are codependent on one another, or substances, that is learned behavior. If they have low self-esteem, undiagnosed mental illness, if there are constant highs and lows, you will seek out or create your own drama to feel the crash afterward. The impact of learned behavior is limitless, and trying to figure it out is the first step. If there are things that just don't sit right with you, or you find yourself repeating bad habits, you need to figure out where those habits started. There is no one to blame in life. We all must realize that no one is perfect and parenting is the hardest job on the planet. We are all juggling jobs, relationships, and financial responsibilities, and throwing children into the mix is crazy.

Unlearning bad behaviors and coping mechanisms is a process, as is life. Life is a journey, not a fifty-meter dash. Most of us want a quick fix to solve everything, a magic pill, instant gratification, but this is unrealistic. When going on a healing journey, especially if there was trauma growing up, learned behaviors are rooted in places that most of us have hidden away in fear. Facing your fears, going through the process, realizing that you are worth it, and realizing that we are all here for a reason is a great start. Knowing you are worth it, will over time, become second nature. As you go through the process of loving yourself, you realize that you can never give up on yourself. You will have bad days, but you must keep going, and you will get there.

Each of the steps will build onto themselves. There will be setbacks, but those setbacks can be learning tools to figure out where to go next. If something triggers you to relapse into an old version of yourself, then you need to process your experience and figure out why it triggered you and how to change your reaction to it so that you do not stay stuck in old patterns. There are always going to be things that pop up in life to challenge us. There is no smooth sailing; life throws curve balls to make sure that you are on track. For if life was predictable, it would be hard to figure out if we were actually growing or changing.

This may seem vague. We all have our own issues to resolve, but the more you can figure out about yourself, the more the path will unfold for you. As long as you keep taking steps of patience and perseverance, you will get there. What works for me may not work for you; we are all in different places in our lives and finding five minutes a day to meditate or journal may be difficult. The whole point is making the time for yourself. Even this statement, if you are saying it to yourself, is a learned behavior. If you cannot find time to work on yourself, more than likely your parents did not find time for you.

Healing yourself is not a journey to perfection. It is a search for the place where we are content with who we are, where we have learned to love and accept ourselves and our idiosyncrasies.

Contentment is one of those things that we overlook these days. We live in a fast-paced world and forget that life in itself is a miracle. We forget that the ones who run the fastest on the hamster wheel are the ones with the most to run from. Being content in your own skin and with what you have is, itself the essence of being you.

This is the time to learn patience with yourself and to persevere through the obstacles. Sometimes it will feel like you are swimming through mud and not getting anywhere, but then, all of a sudden, the lightbulb will go off and you will be exactly where you are meant to be.

CHAPTER 4

Mirror

When I talk about turning the mirror around, it is not to look at the image in the mirror, but into the soul behind your eyes. It's about self-reflection, to see who you are, the good, the bad, the ugly, and everything in between. Are you living your true self, or are you wearing masks to be who others want you to be?

Believe me: it is not an easy task to turn the mirror around to truly see yourself. We need to do this often over the course of our lives. There is one thing I need to clarify; your physical being is just a vessel for your soul. The vessel caries the lineage baggage from your parents and ancestors. Your soul is your intuition, your time traveler of existence. If you only see the external and never delve into the internal, than you have some work to do.

Society is obsessed with the exterior and is self-mutilating to attempt to fit the perfect image. I have met people who are beautiful on the exterior but completely ugly human beings inside. Society is so obsessed with the external values that we forget to connect with who is on the inside. We fail to connect at this level with the ones that are right in front of us. Our kids, our spouses, and ourselves. You cannot truly love, until you love yourself. Our kids are withering away from neglect. The important connections that most of them are making, they are getting from a screen. They are mimicking what they see their parents and loved ones do in front of them. They are disconnecting from themselves and from you. Parents in general need to take a step back and take responsibility for their children and their children's rights. The education system has become glorified daycare; it is not there to educate our children, but to fill their minds with what the government thinks they should learn.

Back to turning the mirror around. If there is something that you see that you do not like, then change it. Remember that you should be looking into your soul, not your bodies reflection. If you are ignoring yourself or your kids, if you are constantly arguing, if you berate yourself and constantly judge yourself and others, it time to self-reflect about your life. If you have addictions—food, alcohol, sex, gambling, and so on, if you are not treating yourself or your loved ones around you properly, then figure out how to make the changes for you first. Taking care of yourself first is not selfish; it is a necessity. For you are going to spend the rest of your life with you.

The book *Women Who Love too Much* shows you the learned patterns we have all inherited and offers suggestions on how to change them. Change can only come from you. This is something that you must want to do for yourself. No one can make the changes for you; there is no magic little pill that is going to fix you. In my profession, it is one of the hardest things for me to wrap my mind around. Most people are looking for everyone to fix them. These are also the same people who blame everyone for what is wrong with them.

Life does not come with a manual; we must make this remarkable journey on our own. There is good and bad in all of us. It is your choice which one you will allow to guide your path. We all have danced with the dark side only to realize that we would rather be in the light. There are always going to be dark days, but, over time, if you work for you, they become less frequent.

CHAPTER 5

Trust

Trust is something that you learn. If you were not nurtured as a child, you will not develop trust. Trust is something that you must learn from yourself, others, and the universe. Most of us go from living with our parents to living with roommates or a partner. We do not take the time to live on our own and learn to trust ourselves. People are pack animals, and now everyone seems to be following the herd. In doing so, we never really learn to navigate on our own. This ability is essential throughout life, for down the road, if a spouse dies, or you become empty nesters, you will find yourself lost. If one of your learned behaviors is codependency, being alone might be tricky at first but learning how to trust yourself will definitely be worth it as time goes on.

Learning to listen to your own intuition and making decisions on your own is a vital part of trusting yourself. It also teaches you how to trust others. If you do not trust yourself, you may trust anyone that comes along, thinking that they have your best interests at heart, when they don't. As you learn to love yourself, you will understand how you want to be treated—with love and respect. The same goes with trust. As we teach ourselves unconditional love, knowing that we are going to make the right decisions for ourselves is learning to trust ourselves.

All things take time, if you think about how long it has taken to learn negative behaviors, unlearning will take some time, but where do you have to go? Life is not a race, it is a journey, and learning tools to better yourself is a gift to yourself—embrace it. You will thank yourself as things become easier for you. Trusting the universe is encompassing all the things we have learned, listening to intuition, and getting in touch with your soul. Your soul is the time traveler of your existence. Your soul chose this vessel and life that you are currently living before you were ever born. Things are already laid out for you; it is up to you which roads you take along the way. Trying to control all the things in your life will not work and is not necessary. If you listen and trust the process, the universe will guide.

Believe me: relinquishing control to the universe took me some time to wrap my head around. The amount of stress you are going to put on yourself by trying to control something that is predestined is unbelievable. You are literally fighting your own existence. It is like watching salmon swimming upstream to spawn—some make it, some don't, but the destination is the same. The more you try to control everything, the more your life will become derailed. You will feel unhappy and depressed; these are signs that you are not following your true path. We all have a purpose on this planet; once you slow down and listen, you will find out what that purpose is.

CHAPTER 6

Relationships—Know Yourself

aving money or status does not give anyone the right to treat you differently. Money does not buy happiness. It does not guarantee perfect relationships or happy children. True happiness is often harder to find if you have a lot of money since there are often expectations that go along with it. If you are working all the time, your relationships take the back seat and so does your health and your overall well-being. This tends to make people irritable. Life is about balance, having enough money so that we can enjoy our lives. I watched my father work seven days a week for the majority of his life; he retired at sixty-eight and died the next year. He did not get to enjoy any of what he sowed, nor did he know how to, for all he knew was how to do was work.

There are a lot of stories of people with lots of money who died alone in the end because they treated everyone terribly along the way to reaching their success and power and had no time for lasting relationships. If we slow down and develop a relationship with ourselves, the relationships that we develop with others will be stronger and filled with love. Once you start on your own healing journey, your time becomes invaluable, and you will only want to share it with like individuals.

Maintaining positive relationships is key, if you stay stuck in negative relationships you will get sucked back into that way of thinking, here are some of examples of negative and positive energy, which you can apply to yourself, or the ones around you.

Examples of negative energy include dishonesty, selfishness, complaints, sadness, laziness, jealousy, confusion, hatred, procrastination, superficiality, worry, self-centeredness, ego, arrogance, greed, ignorance, anger, violence, indifference, loneliness, and insecurity.

Examples of positive energy include generosity, forgiveness, honesty, trust, calmness, love, motivation, gratitude, efficiency, passion, happiness, bravery, joy, inspiration, loyalty, selflessness, forethoughtfulness, diligence, kindness, creativity, responsibility, supportiveness, confidence, and peacefulness.

Negative thoughts can be learned behaviors depending on the environment you were raised in, and the environment you are currently living in. Negativity can be swirling around in your head. Finding a mantra to change your thoughts into positivity is imperative. (I will list a few of my favorite mantras at the end of this book to get you started.) You literally must retrain yourself to think and react in a new way. Releasing negativity is part of this journey. Most of the negativity is probably not yours at all, but baggage you have been carrying from others. Learning to trust yourself and your own intuition will become easier as you learn to nurture yourself and resolve your issues. This is not going to happen overnight; it is a journey you need to embrace. Embrace opening yourself up to vulnerability. Being vulnerable to yourself is a huge learning tool. Feeling and releasing emotions can be overwhelming, especially when they are deep-rooted from childhood.

Nurturing yourself and your inner child is very important, and differentiating between childhood issues and adult reality is key. Figuring out the layers of yourself is how you figure out where and how you need to heal. Journaling timelines and recognizing patterns will help you figure out if you are being triggered by something that you have buried. Finding a good therapist to get you over the hump will definitely help. They can guide you or direct you to resources to figure things out. Or just cry your frustrations out in the middle of your living room, take a walk in nature, or a drive in your car while screaming at the world. I am trying to put a lot of suggestions out there, so that if you cannot afford to go to therapy, there are avenues that you can take to get you where you need to go.

I personally like to figure out things on my own, so that they are my thoughts, not someone else's opinions which might cloud my own judgement. I like to putter around, distract my brain, then usually the clarity comes. If you sit and dwell on things, the hamster on the wheel just runs faster. Keeping busy by doing things that you like to do, and that are positive for you and your environment will help you sort things out. Simple things can distract you so your brain can slow down and focus on something other than the stress. Worrying will not help you in the long run. It just robs you of valuable time now.

Changing up your routine is also a good way to change things in a more positive manner. Start off your day differently, go for a walk, meditate, clean your space. Having tidy surroundings helps so that there are not so many distractions. This is part of nurturing yourself. Having a clean space to start and end your day will make things flow more smoothly. If your life is in chaos but your surroundings are tidy, it will help to calm you. Having a checklist also helps; as we get stressed, we tend to let things we need to deal with pile up, and this becomes overwhelming. If you can make a list and check off a few things each day, the load becomes lighter. Plus, checking things off your list is also a good distraction from the hamster wheel in your mind.

Getting a proper night's sleep, feeding yourself healthy foods, and having positive people in your life, are all good ways to invoke positive change. If you cannot find positive people, then be one, and limit the time you spend with the negative. Learning to be alone with yourself is an amazing thing, and it is OK to crave alone time. We live in a society where everyone is trying to connect with everyone else, and we forget to connect with ourselves. Sitting in a quiet space, listening to your own breath, is a healing tool we can all utilize. Your breath is your life force, and it is also your soul; your soul is your guiding force, your intuition. We all need to listen to her and connect with her. Your soul is your true essence of self, connecting with your soul and not just with your physical self is who you are. Your soul is the time traveler of existence; she has been there with you from lifetime to lifetime. Man, woman, and everything in between, we are not necessarily the same sex in every lifetime. The physical is just that—the *physical*. Your true essence is all-encompassing. Your true sexuality is both male and female; we are all both the yin and yang that reside in us. Don't confuse the physical with who you are. We all must be male and female over the course of our lives. I was a single mom for the majority of my son's life, so I had to play both roles with him. There are always going to be times when you need to be softer or stronger over the course of your existence. If you are lucky enough to dwell in a female body, why would you sacrifice this beautiful creature, trying to keep up with men? We are the creators of life. Without men and women, the human race would no longer exist.

Let us talk about love and relationships; most of us start dating in high school or shortly thereafter. Your prefrontal cortex, the area of the brain that controls long-term decision making, is not yet developed. We still have not left the comfort of our parental home and are jumping in with both feet. Because of instinct, natural progression of life, and what is thought best for us, we have not even got to know ourselves, but we are going hook, line, and sinker for someone else. This is a natural transference of love from parents to a partner. When we have no clue who we are, we tend to give our whole self to someone else, looking for love in return. For most, this falls short, unless you are lucky enough to find your soulmate.

We tend to give ourselves over to another and completely forget about what is best for ourselves. Determined that this relationship is going to work, we give it our all. Things tend to fade, most stop trying as hard, and the honeymoon phase ends. For some it might fizzle out, but for others comes marriage and kids, and then *boom*, a midlife crisis at fifty. We have no idea how we got here. Then we go searching for what is missing—another person, toys, or your own soul. My point to all of this is if we actually took time to get to know ourselves, what we like, what makes us happy, and all of the qualities in ourselves that we like or dislike, we could make better life choices. Letting ourselves develop past our teenage years is important. Getting to know human nature and how it works is key for longevity for our relationships and ourselves.

When you take time to get to know yourself, you will be able to see big red flags in others, the negative qualities that you have healed in yourself, that no longer reside in you. You will pick up on traits in others that do not really meld with your own ideals and morals any longer, remember, like attracts like, but once we heal ourselves, we may not like certain qualities in others any longer. We tend to rush through everything when we are young and wish half our life away on what we think life is supposed to be like instead of just going along for the ride.

If we did not receive the love that we needed as children, then we seek to fill that void inside of us from an external source. Like attracts like, so more than likely you will meet someone with very similar circumstances as yourself. When the honeymoon phase fades, now the relationship has become more of a habit, for you have never lived alone, and you get stuck. If you are with someone you love, then they will understand that you need time to work on yourself, so even if it is five minutes after you drop the kids off, just breath in your car, try new things on your own.

When my son was a toddler, I started doing yoga; it was a ninety-minute class that I could escape to. It's a world where I could focus on me. If you do not focus in yoga, you will fall over, so this was a great thing for me for it allowed my brain to shut off for the class and focus on something other than the world around me. Each week I got stronger and started feeling better and eventually added another class a week. Now I do my practice at home with an app. For it fits into my life so much easier, and I can do it when I can fit it in. I try to get on my mat at least four times a week.

Connecting with yourself is key, and once you start to find that five minutes a day, you will realize how crucial it is for your overall well-being and will want to add more time for you. If you really look at the big picture of your life, how happy you are and what is missing, building a relationship with yourself is vital. If you are running on the hamster wheel, figure out where you can cut out some things to actually focus on you. Unload toxic relationships, whether that be with friends or family. As you are doing this, question yourself why they are toxic. With most relationships, like attracts like. In the beginning of a relationship, the good qualities pull you in, but if things progress in a negative manner, then figure out why. Is it something you do not like, is it the way you are being treated? Is it something in their character that turns you off? People in our lives are a reflection of ourselves. If you do not like it in someone else, then that is something you need to change in yourself.

As we begin to learn to love ourselves, we will see ourselves and the people around us differently. When you start seeing yourself in others, this is a positive thing; it means the work you are doing with yourself is paying off. Not everyone is meant to be in your life forever; you do not need a million friends when you are a friend to yourself. Letting go of toxic relationships is like a tree losing it leaves—it is shedding layers of yourself that are no longer needed so something new will grow and develop in its place.

If you are searching for that one person to change your life, take a look in the mirror.

As I keep saying, we are all a work in progress. Some of us will never change. You cannot change anyone but yourself. As you grow and nurture yourself, you will step into your own power, and I do not mean control and dominance. Your own power is that of being comfortable in your own skin, trusting yourself and the universe to make the right decisions, and having confidence from within that exudes outward. You will be beautiful in a whole different way than you were before. Know your self-worth, put all the blocks of yourself together, and build a rock-solid foundation with the ease of knowing that no matter what comes along, you will be able to weather the storm.

CHAPTER 7

Love

There were so many things wanted to discuss in this book that it was hard to know where to start. I believe that the holy grail of life is love. The most important thing is love, the answer to global warming is love, the answer to war is love, and the answer to so many of us being broken is love. During COVID-19, when we had so much time to think, I was hoping this would be something that most of us would realize, but nope. As soon as restrictions were lifted, everything went back to the norm, like COVID-19 never existed.

Accept that we all do not need to be rich and famous to make a difference on this planet. Good human beings are few and far between these days. If we all just stay numbed out or believe that we cannot make an impact, nothing will change. We need love and good intentions to change for a brighter future.

Accepting that love is the one thing we have not tried on a global level starts with us. Women are primarily the nurturers. Our children are born from our very existence, so whatever changes you make for yourself will resonant in your children. Actions speak louder than words when it comes to teaching our children. Our children learn by watching and mimicking what they see and hear. That is why it is so important to be aware of familial patterning and to try to change it for the next generation. This is one of the definitions of lineage. There is supposed to be one person in every generation who will make the changes for the future. Why should that person not be you?

That brings me to gratitude. If we can accept who we are right now, then we can be grateful for what we have right now. Being grateful for our health, food to eat, clean water, and hopefully a roof over our heads is all we need. I am grateful for the love in my heart and all around me, even after all of the things I have been through. I have figured out that loving myself is the greatest gift I could have ever given myself. It truly changes how you look at things, how you think about things, and how you view the people around you. When you are truly able to love yourself and accept yourself for all the good and the bad, it will change how you view others. You will see people through different eyes. When you stop judging yourself, you will stop judging others. This allows you to accept people for who they are, not for who you want them to be. You do not need to love every person you come across, but you need to accept the knowledge that everyone has their own story that brought them to where they are today.

There are always going to be people that cannot embrace change for themselves or the people or situations around them. People fear the unknown and are driven by fear, which usually means they stay stuck. The more we can lead by example for the world to see, the less scary it will become for others. The herd right now is traveling toward fear, and we need to change direction to love.

Having a simple life where there is no stress, a job that you love, and the time to love yourself and the ones that surround you is all we need. We only truly need food, water, shelter, and love to exist. Instead, we are killing ourselves for things and lifestyles that do not truly make anyone happy. We are all just pretending that any of it makes us happy. Most of us just want to be home surrounded by the people that love us, or your dog, and be done with it. We have created a fast lifestyle to keep up with people that are no happier than anyone else. We are all truly looking for the same thing—*love*. At the end of a hard day, we all just want to go to a place where we feel loved and supported.

We are all chasing a dream, but what if the dream was right in front of us the whole time—*you*. Why not just find out who you are, all the good, all the bad, and everything in between? Be the love that you want to share with others, find the love in your own heart for yourself before you can give it to another. Why rush anything until you truly know what makes you tick and find that elation of love inside of you? At the end of your days when you are truly surrounded by love, it will be a world that you created all on your own. What an amazing accomplishment that would truly be. Why does a dream have to be a big house, lots of money, and power? Why can it not just be a little place to call your own, filled with love and contentment? Putting the pieces of your own existence together is something only a rare few get to do. Why should it not be for each and every one of us? When we fill ourselves with love, we want to share it with all, and you can. Just by feeling it in your heart, it radiates out to all in existence. That energy that is generated from love will be emitted across time and space. If we can all just leave a legacy of love, what a miracle that would be. If we could join together for one purpose of loving ourselves and this planet to turn things around for the future, what a legacy and an accomplishment for all.

"Learn to differentiate between the sound of your intuition guiding you and your traumas misleading you."

Author Unknown

When you find unconditional love within every cell of your body, it is an elation of emotion, not only for yourself but for human existence and this beautiful planet we get to call home. It is almost orgasmic. To feel love in every cell of your body is the most important gift you can give yourself and humanity. I hope this book can help people to come together, to create energy circles, to go into clearings and join hands, and the loop has to close. The energy that will radiate will put us all, and our planet, into a state of healing. Come to this circle in love not only for yourself but for all of humanity for one hour.

CHAPTER 8

What is Greatness?

What does it mean to achieve greatness in your life? I believe if you can make an impact on just one person during your life, you will have achieved greatness. Whether by being a great mother, friend, lover, sister, or just by being yourself. The opportunity is going to be different for every single one of us, but that is what life is—a journey unto yourself. The biggest thing is to not compare yourself to what you think greatness is for anyone else. Nor should you judge anyone else for their journey. If we can turn to one another in love and kindness, we will all have achieved greatness.

Just to be able to still carry love in your heart after being broken so many times is magnificent. Accomplishments do not have to be splitting the atom, for it has already been done in a world that has been built on war and violence. Maintaining love and peace in your heart is a great accomplishment.

CHAPTER 9

Things Are Bad

Unfortunately, I don't think we realize how detrimental this little government experiment (COVID-19) was to so many people. There are still so many people living in fear. How do you conquer fear? With love.

First let us talk about our medical system, and I am sure it is the same in most countries, where doctors are just treating patients as a list of symptoms and giving them medication to suppress the symptoms. We are a society that has bought in to the concept that snake oil will heal everything. Doctors have leaned on the pharmaceutical industry far too long and have forgotten how to be real doctors. We have forgotten the power of the human body to heal itself if put into the right environment and fed with nutritious foods. We have become lazy in looking after ourselves for we think there is a magical pill to fix us. There is not. Most drugs only treat symptoms and do not correct the source of the problem. Your body will build up an immunity to the effects of most drugs, or the drugs may start to attack your body and break it down. We have relinquished the responsibility for our own health to a profession that is making us sicker due to its dependence on pharmaceuticals.

A little lesson on how things work in your body. Inflammation leads to disease; disease can lead to cancer. What causes inflammation? Emotional stress, physical stress, dietary stress, and environmental stress.

The potential for emotional trauma surrounds us, but if we deal with these issues at the time and not let them fester, we can combat the inflammation. There is a book called *Understanding the Messages of Your Body* by John-Pierre Barrall. This book explains that what your brain cannot process, it dumps into other organs—kidneys hold fear, the liver holds anger, the spleen and pancreas hold low self-esteem, and so on. This book tells you how each organ works, the emotions that it stores, characteristics that go along with it, and some ways to treat the problem. As an example, if you were kicked in the leg by a bully, there is going to be physical trauma at the site of impact but also an emotional response to being bullied. Depending on where you were kicked, there could be a huge amount of tissue damage to the area. If the physical or emotional damage is not treated properly, the memory of the injury can be triggered later because of fear and anger. The inflammation lies dormant and can be reactivated if not dealt with.

We need to start learning a bit more about our bodies so that injuries do not repeat themselves in a crisis. Learning some coping mechanisms and some home remedies is crucial. One of the most detrimental things to our health is stress. Stress weakens your immune system, making you susceptible to viruses or bacteria. Stress correlates to emotional trauma.

As the title states, let's start the conversation. That is what I am hoping this book will do, elicit some difficult conversations, whether that be with yourself or your loved ones. Changing the narrative in our own minds to a more positive loving outlook on life, inclusive of one another, is something we all need to do. Accept that we are all part of the human race. The fact that we all exist at the same time is not by chance; it was mapped out before any of us were even conceived.

Don't get me wrong, I think that having a higher purpose is daunting for many, and we have all been taught to take the easy way in life. Through addiction, self-suppression, feeling that because we were born as women, we cannot stand up and become powerful individuals and still be good moms, human beings, friends, and so on. Men have ruled the world, though many of them are sociopaths. They have suffered no repercussions thus far for it was under the umbrella of government. How is it that over time women have been burned at the stake, institutionalized, and deemed inferior, while men mass murder people for land and power with no repercussions?

I look around and see and hear about so many unhappy people, everyone trying to live up to this false reality that we have created. The expectation is that we are all meant to be rich and famous; we are not. We are all meant to be different but get upset when we don't look the same as our are neighbors or our friends. The entertainment industry was created to distract in times of need—like postwar and economic depression—to cheer up the poor and lift people's spirits. Now we are trying to emulate actors and the rich. But there are not too many people in those groups that are truly happy. Why is it that we are not satisfied with just being who we are without judgement? We have created an unattainable existence. If you are not rich or famous, you are considered inferior. If you are not jet setting, do not have a million friends or some big fancy job, you are not worthy of love. No wonder there are so many unhappy, depressed people on medications or with addictions.

We set ourselves up for failure before we get a chance to figure out who we are. We are sent to school and are supposed to figure out who we want to be for the rest of our lives before our prefrontal cortex is even developed and able retain anything long term.

Then we go off to university to get a degree in something that we may never be able to get a job in. No wonder kids are so confused before they even reach adulthood. Why is it not OK to be happy with just being you? Why do we all have to go to school, get married, get a job, have 2.5 kids, and a dog? For one, the earth cannot sustain any more people, no one wants to work, and 80 percent of marriages end in divorce. If this is your goal, hats off to you and good luck, but if it's not, why not backpack around until you find what you are looking for—*you*. Why do we have to rush into life before any of us are even ready? Why do we expect or want our children to end up like us—depressed, anxious, and unhappy? Why not let our kids forge a new existence of peace and love? Live like tree huggers and help to heal our planet. We don't need more consumerism or industry or trips to the moon; we need to heal our planet and ourselves.

If you look at the big picture, all the things that are killing us are just things that are making some industry or individual richer. All of our systems are broken, and all of our systems have just made us more dependent on the almighty dollar. Our medical system is making us sicker with pharmaceuticals whose effects we have little knowledge of. Our government is terrible, encouraging the young to become dependent on welfare, medicine, and mental health care because keeping people suppressed makes them easier to control. Politicians' campaign platforms are never followed through on once elected. We have stopped taking responsibility for ourselves and have instead put our lives into the hands of ego-driven men that just want to line their pockets. If we lived in peace and harmony, we would not need politicians in the roles they are currently holding. If we lived in a place of love and happiness, we would no longer need the medical system as it is today. We are getting sicker because we are all stressed out dying for change.

CHAPTER 10

Planet

To save our planet, we need to revise our way of thinking. We do not own this earth. Sure, we may occupy space, but in the end, she will take us all out if we do not start changing the energy that we give back to her. War has not worked. Einstein has defined insanity as doing the same thing over and over and expecting different results. If you look at the earth now from the outside, it is just a bunch of spoiled little boys who never played nice in the sandbox. Now they are playing a game of risk with the fate of us all in their hands.

It is time to try something new. It is time to have a global purpose of like mindedness to save this beautiful place called Mother Earth. It is time to live in peace and harmony. If we all put our heads together and spread the energy of love and kindness, we will no longer accept the government as it is.

If we change our global mindset and realize that this planet gives us, the human race, all we need to survive, then we might start to give back instead of raping and pillaging. We can build a stronger planet. Energy is something that we are all talking about. It is inside of us; we are energy. Every cell in your body is energy. Everything in nature is energy; we have this in common. There is a magnetic field that surrounds the earth that resonates at the same frequency as our hearts at rest.

Look at the changes that occurred when we all experienced the first year of COVID-19. The world began to recover back to a place of balance. Then when restrictions were lifted, we all could not wait to get out and travel and go back to the old way of living. The earth began to deteriorate again. We have been broken for centuries; it is time to try something new. We need to simplify our lives to give back to this beautiful planet.

At the same time, the energy created globally will heal everyone and this planet. It will be the start of world peace and love for all living breathing entities on this planet. It will be the most powerful thing that any of us will ever experience in our existence. If you can get to a clearing, do it with your neighbor, your friends, or your family. Go somewhere outside and you will all feel the energy generated from one another. If you are alone, find a group that you have never seen before and join in, for the energy will be an out-of-body sensation. It will be the day that slows down out of love and positivity instead of fear from a globally constructed pandemic. The way to conquer your fears is through love. How can you not feel that when we all join together in love? It will change the course of time and the energy fields that surround us. To resonate peace on a global scale will reverberate through the earth's core and put her at the peace she has been longing for. For if it was not for Mother Earth, none of us would be in existence today. This is the foundation of the future that we want to create for ourselves and generations to come. Love will be the start of a healing process that no one has ever experienced because we have lived in fear of the unknown since existence began. Love is what we are all created for. We are all meant to be here at this moment to change the human race through love and gratitude. If we all start an ohm chant from the depths of our souls, it will put things into a balance that we have never experienced before. This is my hope for all humanity.

I believe in each and every person who is willing to wear their heart on their sleeve for mankind. I love and thank you.

Men have not got it right thus far ruling the world; I think it is time to change our future for the better. Also, when coming together to support Mother Earth, it just seems right that it will be women who figure out how to truly support and love this beautiful planet we coexist with. She gave us life. Now it is time to give life back to her.

We do not own this planet. She owns us and will destroy us if we do not step up to make the changes she is longing for, what we are all longing for—an existence of love, peace, prosperity, and trust. This planet normally nurtures and rejuvenates, but now she is pissed because we are not listening. We can change that by cleaning house of ego, greed, and destruction. Having a united purpose gives us all something to work toward. It is time to stand together as the entire human race instead of black, white, or whatever label you can fill in here. Love will unify us all as we love ourselves and love our existence on this planet we call home.

I know I have geared this book toward women but this is for everyone. We are all a little broken and need to take a step back to look at why. Looking at everything in a big picture, there is no need to fight anymore. We have established laws, formed governments, a medical system, and a welfare system, all of which are broken down. For they were established when we were all living in fear and were uneducated. Times have changed for most of us. Now that we have different cultures living everywhere, there are no borders to human kindness. We know the difference between right and wrong. We have the capability to look after ourselves. There is no reason we should all be living in fear. The only thing to fear now is the egomaniacs that are residing in government and the puppet master that is behind all of it. If we can stand up for ourselves, and learn to love ourselves, we will no longer be doormats to the system. When we realize that, it becomes way more important to be the generation that makes the changes to save our planet. We can let go of the idea that we all need to be rich and famous and concentrate on changes that will impact us all.

I believe in the human race; I see in us all the love that is waiting to pour out and heal the world, we just need to find that key to unlock the gate that we have all built to protect ourselves. We have everything we need to move forward together: food, water, shelter, and love. We also have technology to make the changes needed to give back to this planet instead of sucking her dry. We need to clean our water. In Canada we have the largest fresh water supply in the world. We need to stop polluting it and figure out a filtration system that will help keep our water supply pure. We need to stop feeding our land sites with garbage, stop littering, and start giving back with regenerative farming. We need to start putting our heads together instead of sitting in little boxes trying to be the next Einstein, we need to work together to heal this planet. If we can do this, we all will win.

We all need to take responsibility for our lives and our world and be held accountable. We cannot keep blaming everything on someone or something else. Your decisions today define your tomorrow. Time to stand up, dust yourself off, and try again. Most of us do not have a purpose anymore, we end up like a dog chasing its tail, ending up nowhere. If we have a global goal to save our planet, it gives us a purpose for change. The change must start from within. Our purpose will also give people the feeling of togetherness. There are so many lost souls wandering because they do not feel connected anymore. The feeling of community has been lost; it is every man for himself. Instead, we need to work together and help one another. Mental illness is on the rise, for we are all driving ourselves crazy trying be perfect and create the perfect image, trying to fit into this image of what we think life is supposed to look like. We have gotten so far away from reality that we are driving ourselves crazy searching for an existence that is unattainable.

We are looking up to people because of the money and fame they possess. But the truth is none of these people are any better off than you or me, we all go through ups and downs in life. There is no perfection. Growth means change, and we do not all grow together. Contentment within yourself should be what we are all striving for instead of the false ideals of a "perfect life." We are becoming robots and sheep in a delusional society.

Gratitude for what we have, who we are, and where we are, should be the mantra of life. This should be our prayer at the end of day. We have fresh air to breath, food and water, a beautiful planet to call home, and someone to love.

We all need to sacrifice some time to give back to Mother Earth. During the first year of COVID-19 when the earth stopped, nature started repairing herself. We need to figure out how to slow the process of global warming, sacrifice travel, and regulate population growth. The biggest thing that is killing our planet Is the number of people residing on her. We need to give up the idea that we all need to live forever. Our souls are the time travelers; we need to wrap our heads around that and save our planet for the next life.

Again, we must hold ourselves accountable. If you want to be a corporate somebody that works sixteen hours a day, don't have kids.

If you find yourself in a life of addiction, don't have kids. If you are not in a good place within yourself, wait to have kids. Children are our future, and they need to be cherished and nurtured. If you cannot do that, then wait until you can. Taking time to figure out your shit is a very responsible thing to do. Realizing that we all do not need to look the same or lead the same lives is strength. Being an individual who is making responsible decisions for a better tomorrow is power. Inner power and strength are priceless, and not everyone is utilizing the gifts that are inside of themselves. The holy grail we are seeking is locked inside of us all. We are all just so consumed with the thought that it is something that exists outside of ourselves. There is no hidden treasure or pot of gold at the end of the rainbow; the hidden treasure is within you. You are the pot of gold, and that is the search that we all need to be on. Look for the holy grail within you.

As I said earlier about cellular connections and genetic links, we have to decipher the code that is inside of us. What is truly us, and what baggage we are carrying from our history. When fighting your demons, you need to figure out which part is you and which is cellular memory from our mothers and previous generations. Deciphering the code and becoming you is the journey of life. A journey that is as unique as you.

Your decisions today define your tomorrow. You can choose to stay down or get back up with grace and elegance. Redefine who you are, and should have been, all along. We are powerful creatures, which is why we are the ones who give life. I think that we have forgotten how much of a miracle and a gift that life truly is.

As we heal ourselves on an individual level, that energy will resonate to the collective. Energy fields are endless, and as each of us goes through the phases of healing, the effects will be felt by all. Some of you may have noticed that in the last few years, the collective energy has been very negative, and at times, it has been difficult to keep a positive outlook. If we all start on our journey of healing and well-being, how magnificent that energy will be. The most magnificent will be when we reach a collective of letting go of all learned behavior, conditioned behavior, ego etc. Individually, this is one of the most progressive stages of growth, but as a collective for humanity, it will mean letting go of centuries of fear, control, ego, power, and unworthiness. In its place will rise bliss, contentment, love, and gratitude for ourselves, for each other, and for Mother Earth. We will all be able to breathe with ease knowing what we were all sent here to do. Our purpose is to heal ourselves, this planet, and our beautiful universe. This is the holy grail that we are all seeking.

For humanity to live and exist in a state of gratitude is a collective soul journey for all. This is why we keep coming back (resurrection), to get it right. Each step we take with a unified purpose will create the building blocks of a utopian existence. To exist in peace will supply the energy we need to heal and calm Mother Earth, to quiet that anger from her core that is disrupting our climate. She is no longer whispering to get our attention; she is now screaming in our ears that we need to listen. Are we going to pay attention or are we going to stay in a state of ego and denial to the only thing that truly matters for our future, Mother Earth?

We have the technology and knowledge to realize that we cannot exist in outer space for long periods of time. Even if we could, only a fraction of us would want such a terrible existence. A future without trees, water, nature, seasons, and rain. Without early morning coffee and sunsets. No first snowfalls on Christmas morning. No long strolls on the beach, walks in the park, skiing, or mountains. One thing I know we could not take with us is our four-legged friends; I cannot imagine a life without them. These are the memories I want everyone to experience beneath their feet and in their lungs.

So let us start the conversations we have all been avoiding, too afraid to initiate, and plan a future of love and gratitude for ourselves for a better future. Forget the past and the mistakes we have made thus far. Move forward with ease and contentment for a brighter future for every generation to come, for all living breathing creatures that makes this planet whole.

The conversation needs to be gentle and quiet, no more fighting, no one is right or better at this stage of the game, for none of us has experienced a world without fear and hate. If we all take a deep breath and move forward in ease and grace, we can put our hearts together to forge a beautiful path to a brighter more beautiful future for all in existence, today, tomorrow, and always.

I will write another book, but I think we all need to process this one first. We need to contemplate what is important and put our past behind us, leave our egos at the door, take a walk in nature, and actually try to fathom a future if we keep destroying the planet, for she will destroy us if we keep going in this direction. Everything has led us to this point in time; sit back, self-reflect, and look at the pieces of history that have brought us here. The one that sticks in my mind is a quote from Albert Einstein: "The definition of insanity is doing the same thing over and over and expecting a different result."

Do we really want to kill ourselves for another world war that will only lead to another ice age, or whatever end Mother Nature has for us, if we keep repeating history.

I have such hope in humanity, and I see this hope in the eyes of everyone I pass. Everyone is looking for that answer that we all have lurking inside of ourselves—love.

I wish you all good luck on this next part of your journey, for it will bring us to a place where we can trust our souls to guide us in the right direction, and we can trust in the right people to help navigate our future. Let us start the conversation.

This book is my heart, my hope, my dream, and my soul. I know that in all my lives I have been a healer, I have been all cultures, and I have been both sexes. In this life, I am a strong, attractive woman who tells her story so that people will listen. There is a saying, "women should lift the crowns of others," but it is more that we need to lift our own crowns so we can lift others. If we can learn to heal ourselves, we will no longer need medications and war; we can start to give back to ourselves, to others, but mostly to Mother Earth.

My hope is that in my next lifetime there is no longer a need for my services as a healer for we will all be able to do this for ourselves.

Acknowledgements

Thank you to Lynda Mickleborough for all your help structuring my words and most of all our friendship, thank you to my sisters, and my son for guiding me through unconditional love.

Mantras

I am love, I have love, and I am loved.

I am enough; I release what no longer serves me.

I trust the timing and unfolding of my life.

I am exactly where I need to be.

Thank you, [add your own gratitude].

Rooted in my power, opened through my heart,

I surrender to all that is here to heal me.

I am safe, I am grounded, and I am rooted

to the loving vibration of my being.

Some of My Quotes

Find your voice in your heart.

Be confident in your decisions.

I am no longer willing to ride the hamster wheel of life.

Loving myself has opened my eyes to

the love that surrounds me.

Printed in the USA
CPSIA information can be obtained
at www.ICGtesting.com
JSHW010546050224
56524JS00001B/5